Gardeners Do It With Their Hands Dirty

poems by

Robert Knox

Finishing Line Press
Georgetown, Kentucky

Gardeners Do It With Their Hands Dirty

Copyright © 2017 by Robert Knox
ISBN 978-1-63534-208-6 First Edition
All rights reserved under International and Pan-American Copyright Conventions.
No part of this book may be reproduced in any manner whatsoever without written permission from the publisher, except in the case of brief quotations embodied in critical articles and reviews.

ACKNOWLEDGMENTS

The following poems have been published in *Verse-Virtual*:
"The Tiny Beak the Flower Bends," "At Wollaston Beach," and "My 'Little Girl Dreams'" [http://www.verse-virtual.com/robert-c-knox-2014-december.html]
"Outdoor Living," "Parsing of Names," "Human Bee-ing," "The Garden Czar," "The Scripture of Nature," "The Name of the Flower," and "Consider the Bee" [http://www.verse-virtual.com/robert-c-knox-2015-january.html]
"My Dad's Ship But One Of Three," "Family Secrets"
[http://www.verse-virtual.com/robert-c-knox-2015-february.html]
"The Sacred Way" and "Boat Ride for Mom"
[http://www.verse-virtual.com/robert-knox-2016-july.html]
"Commanding the Sun" was published by *Rain, Party & Disaster Society* [http://www.rpdsociety.com/latestissue]
"The Garden of Impermanence" and "Winter Comes to Quincy" were published by Earl of Plaid [http://www.earlofplaid.com/uploads/2/6/2/4/26247627/royal_purple_final.pdf]
"Hot Shots" was published in *The Semaphore* April 2015
[https://yoursemaphorecontent.wordpress.com/]
"Spring Greens Are the Earth's Wild Songs" was published in *These Fragile Lilacs* Vol. 1, issue November 2015 [thesefragilelilacspoetry.com]
"Gardeners Do It With Their Hands Dirty" was published in *Guide to Kulchur Creative Journal* December 2015
"Sidewalk Madonnas" was published in *Off the Coast* Winter 2016; [http://www.off-the-coast.com/OTC_winter2016-contributor-notes.html]
"The Slow Tritina" published in *Yellow Chair Review*, Issue 7, July 2016; [http://www.yellowchairreview.com/single-post/2016/06/20/The-Slow-Tritina-We-Will-Dance]

Publisher: Leah Maines
Editor: Christen Kincaid
Cover Art: From Author's Collection
Author Photo: From Author's Collection
Cover Design: Elizabeth Maines McCleavy

Printed in the USA on acid-free paper.
Order online: www.finishinglinepress.com
         also available on amazon.com

Author inquiries and mail orders:
Finishing Line Press
P. O. Box 1626
Georgetown, Kentucky 40324
U. S. A.

Table of Contents

Part I: Garden Lover

The Tiny Beak the Flower Bends 1
Outdoor Living 2
Parsing of Names 3
Human Bee-ing 5
The Garden Czar 6
The Scripture of Nature 7
The Name of the Flower 8
Consider the Bee 9
The Garden of Impermanence 10
Hot Shots 11
What Happened Today 12
Poem: My Aching Back 13
Commanding the Sun 14
Spring Greens Are the Earth's Wild Songs 16
The Leaf Washers 17
Gardeners Do It With Their Hands Dirty 19

Part II: Places and People

On the Sidewalk at Wollaston Beach 21
Sidewalk Madonnas 24
My 'Little Girl Dreams' 25
The Sacred Way 27
Boat Ride for Mom 28
Old Wooden Doors 30
Winter Comes to Quincy 31
Waiting for the Perseids 32
My Dad's Ship But One of Three 33
Family Secrets 35
The Slow Tritina 36

Part I: Garden Lovers

The Tiny Beak the Flower Bends

The hummingbird
Knows what time it is
Time to be doing
Efficient as day
She collects what the world has to offer
She is a worker of time, paid by the hour
She has no hours to waste
She blazes her tiny light, burns for the blossom
Seizes the day in her needle-point proboscis
Inspects, rejects, takes where she finds it
Shops a garden in a minute, rages hungry for the next
Flies the tiny skies of creation toward the paradise of tomorrow
Migrates hundreds of miles, wings whirring beyond the odometers of man—
Creation's fool!
To the haven of eternal flowers, the honey and the flame

I am the shadow who brings light to the day
The breathless watcher
The anchor in the sea of time
The moving finger who writes the day
The background, the contrast, the negative who lets the picture fly
The giver of dirt, the worshiper
The rootless eye that passes over the land
Like a face upon the water
The lover of the light, the freedom of the wing

The hummingbird
Knows what time is flown
To turn her green breast
To the flowers of the sun

Part I: Garden Lovers

Outdoor Living

We make of nature another room.
A big room if we have a big space,
an ordinary room if the space is small.
Make it comfortable, decorate a little
Make a place to sit. A place to eat.
A place to cook, conditions permitting,
The sun shining, the breezes light—
All this works best if the weather is right
Here's a clue, for me and you—
Wait for the sun to warm things up
Warm is desirable for living outdoors
Warm is "natural," room temperature outdoors
Come on out (or in?)
Look, we have company: It's the Plant Family!
They come in uninvited
Work with them
We can't beat them even if we tried
We want to make a difference
Something beautiful will grow up between us
See? What did I just say?
It's starting, we can't escape it
We too are made of earth
We want to live outdoors
Pass the wine, pick the strawberries
Drop your fig leaf, honey,
You have dirt beneath your fingernails.

Part I: Garden Lovers

Parsing of names

Covered in a sticky substance
You get *stigma* on your nose

Petals attract insects
Be more bee-like
Follow the guidelines

The *style* varies in length
I'll say

The *ovary* will become the fruit
How like life

The *ovule* is like the egg
But it wants to be a seed

The *receptacle* hugs the *stem*
Throw something in there
Pull a strawberry out

Down below is the *nectary*,
Sugar, sugar bowl for insects

Sepals do security
Hey, *bud*, get growing

Filament: this is the stalk of the author—
No—"*anther*"!

And the *anther* is?
Long.

Short answer: *anther, pollen sacs, insect, stigma* (here or somewhere else in town: no one can make a rule for insects),
ovule, fertilization.

Bottom line?

Part I: Garden Lovers

Yes, there are female parts: *stigma, style, ovary, ovule;* known collectively as the *carpel*
And male parts: *filament, anther,* together called *stamen.*
As in most groups, there are more of the females.

Please click to print for children.

Part I: Garden Lovers

Human Bee-ing

Flowers are the sex organs
Of hot momma nature.
We all love the colors, the shapes,
The delicate constructions.
They bring us together.

Do not ask what makes
that deep, persistent buzz
that hovers above Zouave jackets and bell-flared trousers,
transparent angel wings extended,
and wiggles its butt between stamen and pistil
It's us

Part I: Garden Lovers

The Garden Czar

A new campaign, a new front.
I am moving peoples, tribes. Colonies.
I bid them pick up all that they own and journey to the land
which I have prepared for them, or will,
when I have finished dumping them by the roots into a plastic pail,
and take up my oversized hand trowel for the next thrust in world building.
I am, at times, a careless God.
Still, my people will long remember the adventures of this day
and speak of them for generations to come.
(Every spring, I am confident, is a new generation.)
I am the Czarist factotum who tells Tevye and his village to clear out by Friday:
Orders from the top.
Of course I am also the top.

Part I: Garden Lovers

The Scripture of Nature

Some nonchalant immortal turns the page to autumn
On cue, sweet day slips off her shawl, growing warm, sultry, reminiscent
The husband walks the garden in shirtsleeves, thinking of nothing
Everything is semi-shade now, the sun at half-mast
The Morning Glory explores its name
Blooms clinging to the house like a band of nervous orphans
Blood-purple asters peak, already penciling in their winter vacation
(Somewhere you won't see them)
The toad lilies not yet ready to change their spots
A single cricket keeps up a cracked tenor solo—
    a late phase song: he's studied all the great romantics
Give him a few more degrees of autumn's comeback love
And he makes up with the universe: *gotta sing! gotta sing!*
High up in the gathering season a squirrel beeps his barking little horn
squawking at the cat, black and disinterested, who plays possum with time
And so it is written
That a walk in a garden is a prayer routine
Natural places are "thought sinks":
Emotion sinks, agitation sinks.
They absorb the world's disturbances.

Walking on the equipoise of the year,
We tread like garden monks of peerless devotion,
But who invited that tacky squirrel?

Part I: Garden Lovers

The Name of the Flower

Anemone. It's the name that speaks to me,
The name that is its own poem.
When all else fails, a single green plant begins to flower
Pink, daisy-shaped, soft fleshy ears around a clock face of yellow
Coming so late; a message from another world
Buds round and puffy before they open.
With such buds you know what is coming
You wait, like a lover, for the sensuous unfolding,
A prolonged anticipation of the moment.
Do not (a voice tells me) make love to a flower.

But it's timing, as in music, as in love, that lands the punch.
September: the turn in the year,
The turn in the poem of earth.

Not so showy as some,
They keep their heads down
No one calls them "cheerful, sun-loving"
But deep-feeling, hearty, September's half-light loving
They smile, contemplatively
They soak up thoughts too deep for words

Part I: Garden Lovers

Consider the Bee

Consider the honeybee.
How in summer you never see one unmoving
Pollinating the hours in and out of flowers
Now, chilling, they seem to stick to the flower head
As if dead, or frozen, or honey-stuck to the beloved
Soaking up sun, or waiting for it
Soaking up the scent, or nectar of the bloom
Or the fruit and flower, the air itself, the hour, the mind of summer
Wherever a bee may hold such thoughts

So too with us at harvest time
Leaves wheel their colors against a depthless sky.
Apple orchards and rows of black and blue berries the color of dusk

Inhale the bloom, drink in the fruit with your long, pointy eyes,
The lenses of the brain

Part I: Garden Lovers

The Garden of Impermanence

A huge white cumulus, gray in the center, golden at the edges,
floats over the house like a new world, unhurriedly,
to the paradise of the elements.
The wind picks up, the sun is in my eyes.
The wind rises again, rolling the pen.

Another way to title this is: all I want is the pictures.
Point number one. Nothing lasts.
Point number two. There's always tomorrow.

Final line to that poem about flowers,
"The Garden of Impermanence":
Enjoy them while they last.

Part I: Garden Lovers

Hot Shots

In the full New England sun
I'm bleached into a ghost, a limp winding sheet
Do not even imagine
The tropics

The flowers are hot and bright
Some cool green things wilt beside them—
which am I?

I try to capture
On the lens of my brain—
Not to mention the Sony Cyber-Shot
I drag around each day to memorialize the radiance of my best students,
       my garden stars
Like heroes on the gravestones of time

—the quality of air
when no two-leggers are afoot
Even flying things seem quieted
Bees have no buzz this perfectly sweet
and soporific afternoon

The birds are down to
a few scattered postprandial cheeps

And the echoes of man-made engines hovering above
sound merely like the pleasant burbles
of some contented deity at his afternoon nap
dreaming of lazy, self-indulgent days
Will I ever learn such wisdom?

Part I: Garden Lovers

What Happened Today

Blue morning glory.
White impatiens planted last month, in a ring around the weeping cherry tree.
Red impatiens hyper-lit in the sun's first glory.
The fuzzy pinkish Joe Pye-weed, that wild late-season bloomer.
A dark anemone, nearly red, bowed but unbloodied, shadowy from a sun day's overexposure
Pink anemones, enduring, my August friends and companions
Blue Plumbago, in shade. What a rakish name. Is it a dance? A drink? A dish for the daring from a poisonous fish? A shady character?
This year's entry into the praying mantis Hall of Fame for Long Insects. Extended as my hand, turning its face carefully to the side as if to measure my shrinkage. How long before I succeed to dinner?
Two blue morning glory blossoms. Yes, I see them again in the afternoon shadow, outliving their time, famous long ago.
Big hibiscus, pink-lipped and ready for its closeup, but I failed my moment and departed un-kissed.
Dark-pink anemone, back again. Returning with the sun's decline I linger, waiting for your soulful transfusion.
Pink Chablis sedum. This year, this time of year, this seasonal toast.
What happened this September.

Part I: Garden Lovers

Poem: My Aching Back

Bees dart between the streams of spray—
They don't like my rain delays

Bare-stemmed, burned out by the long dry spell
The plants wait patiently for rain

I bend to the task, patience my name
Bearing the heavy pail through twisty garden paths
Aquarius with a sore-point shoulder

A summer day too late for the name
I cheat with the sprinkler
The weary tomatoes rejoice,
flapping their yellow palms and withered phalanges in the spray

A time-worn rain machine
I sit on the borders of my storm
My fountain arcing to the blue

Patter of little foot-drops tom-toming across the hard paths,
stone slices louder than the parched and particled soil

In dreams I chastise my civilized oppressors
begging them at last to step out of doors
and lift their faces to the sky
to drink of the balm that must someday come

Part I: Garden Lovers

Commanding the Sun

Too, too perfect day, an afternoon for the solar
The idyll of the American dream-king
"Everyman a king!" they shouted roaring through the Bastille
Alone in his courtyard, revolutions over
A gardener to himself
He contemplates his next campaign
We will pull up the daisies
And plant only the Spices of Mars!

Did you order this light for the afternoon?
Very good, M. Rudbeckia
A nod to Senor Chard, the Switzer
Very good. A sun for a king.

The king above bathes the king below in light
as he sits on his throne
And who prepared this tableau?
So that even in September, that gentle interregnum
between the festivals of the Summer King and the quick marches of autumn,
shades and contours beguile us
I do not count the ways you love my senses

Hence, rude thoughts of winter!
Summer's blaze a mere crinkling in the radiator
The occasional murmur at the ear only a reminder
Where we have been appears in where we are
The high king's stars mere wrinkles now
Let me contemplate you, darling, without your silks and shawls
Let me see you finally as you are
How long you have been here, underfoot, in my own backyard,
        everywhere I turn *cultiver son jardin*
The buzz in the ear, the time of my life
And why do I keep turning
When the world teaches me to rest,
  with garlands of light, with flowers up my nose, birds in my ears,
        colors wrapped around my eyes?

Part I: Garden Lovers

'Your Majesty, the winds of heaven and hell are at the gate,
   roaring down through the centuries!'
Well, let them in.

The air is free, the light inflicts us, inflects us,
Inflates us, makes us gods
The glory is the moment
The moment does not last and yet is always here
You can't live in the moment—'*Seigneur!*
'They are shouting outside!'—
because it's always disappearing

Then occasionally, when no one is looking,
not even you,
You can

Part I: Garden Lovers

Spring Greens Are the Earth's Wild Songs

  Spring greens are the wild earth's poetry.
  This fresh collection of leaves of grass, line and meter obscured by the pure multitude of all they are.
  They are life's ammunition against the dying of the light,
   the green scatter-shot, the bullets of the universal urge—"urge, urge, always the procreant urge" (to modify a little more Whitman),
    nothing dying, nothing lost, so long as the sun tilts on its celestial shoulder to look back at us,
    turns its face, warm and scented with blossom, pollen, pheromone, hum of the honey bee, the chase of the slap-sparrows over the brown earth of the still unplanted vegetable patch,
   shines upon our raw greenie patch of earth.
   The fire in the senses—the song in the tree
   The neighbor girls bickering in their play, the steady drum-bounce eternal of the Chinese boy's basketball
   The banshee scream electrical, the profanation of the leaf blower (that instrument of the devil)
   The rise and surge of the tiny nations underfoot, violets overblooming their sphere so that anxious fingers pull up handfuls of green hair from beds whose chosen species—think 'nation,' 'clan'—struggles for the breath of light below
    Speedwell, Forget-me-not, Mazus: these names on the lips of ages
    Somewhere Sweet William hides in the weeds
   A green wave invades, overtops the chosen ones, I yank them in the joy of haste, knowing the root remains
   And will overcome in the end, to grow once again over the graves of dying men
   That heads of tulips have fallen in the hurdle of time
    And flowery hands of pansies, over-extended in the friendship of
    air, wait for the clipper
—and so moments, sweet vernal days, and tribes have been lost
   What god looked over our shoulders, blowing hot and cold?
    And yet if not for such days do we live
    To watch the mayfly of understanding
    Flicker in the green light of the new and re-freshed

Part I: Garden Lovers

The renewal of time
The fountain that fills what it overflows
In ancient ecstasy of movement
Of which we drink so long as we live life and
Sense and thirst for its living.

Part I: Garden Lovers

The Leaf Washers
    ("The plants eat light." From Michael Pollan's "How Smart are Plants?" in the New Yorker)

Yesterday we washed the leaves
Today they salute us
Reaching out, waving their storybook lives
Like the pages of a book
Fluttering long fingers
Beckoning, or speaking the gesture language
Heavier creatures invent upon their fingers
They pulse their high wire stories through the air waves

The leaves live in the air, the air is home, shelter, food for them
The current of breath that fills my senses
Orders time for the dance of the hours
The leaves make time for us, filtering the world
The minutes emerge from pores and make sense for us,
Slow as the waves of the world
They save the voices of the children
They lie still before the whine of the engines
To still them is to deafen the magic
They droop like ears silenced by the humdrum of machines
They turn the salutes of the hours into triumphs of air
They sluice and filter the music of the world
They are the companionate senses of the wild green earth,
A bowering neighbor,
A grotto of tuned and tasted pleasure, pre-digested by fertility,
A porous protection, a second self
They guide the sun to my temple
I am—we are—within the village of the world,
Inside temples among the jungled cities
The leaves salute our fellow travelers in their journeys through the sky
As friends, superiors in life, elders, survivors of earlier days
They know where they situate is all the world
They mediate the base of things, the fundamentals,
Molecules, waves, atoms, energy-matter—the rain in Piccadilly,
The fountains of Beirut, the voices of the stars

Part I: Garden Lovers

Gardeners Do It with Their Hands Dirty
> *("You must come to see me," he says. "I will show you my garden." Then when you go, just to please him, you will find him with his rump sticking up somewhere among the perennials...*
> —*from The Gardener's Year, by Karel Capek)*

I do it because it is out of doors
Because I can
Because you can do it alone
And you need—*very little*—but *not nothing*
You need a growing season
(What am I doing in New England?)
I take no prisoners, I take no shit
except out of the manure bag
And you need growing things—creatures willing to grow

(Any volunteers?)

Let me tell you about spring,
When the earth looses its madmen
And ambitions grow like weeds—
No, that would take too long.
Summer, then.
Summer is ravishing, ecstatic, nature on steroids.
Summer is falling in love—wild, messy, overheated.
Lush. Inebriated.
Too damn short.
In addition to which, nothing you do then is ever good enough
To satisfy the wild sense of possibility
you smell like the desire of the stamen for the
honey bee's many hairy legs
... and even if it were, you can't stop time

So at the end, when it's all in the rearview mirror,
Or all in your head—make believe, even—
when you are sobering down with a good glass of hoar frost
And a fresh delivery of number two heating oil...
In the garden, even then, death is beautiful
Autumn is beautiful, like death.
Life is only valuable, remember, because we die

Part I: Garden Lovers

(If you don't believe that, imagine life without flowers,
families without babies)

We are obliged to be happy, as the rabbis tell us
We look at the fading asters, or the Montauk daisies, or the furtive, modest,
ravishing anemone and realize, with some degree of calm,
That we are all on our way (in time) out of time
To the same place
Which, if we are lucky,
Will strongly resemble a garden

In the garden, I know,
That everything is forever and always was
Until it isn't
And even then I'm hedging my bets
Because, understand, there's a garden metaphor for everything,
Even the things we haven't thought of yet

Part II: Places and People

On the Sidewalk at Wollaston Beach

On the sidewalk at Wollaston Beach
people line the seawall taking photos of the moon
We take photos only with our mind,
but we were there first
We are there in the hour before dark
When children, tiny, on tiny bikes
race to the crosswalk of Shoreline Drive
that fury of impatient motors and wait
though the sign says 'walk' they cannot read
too small, but their caretaker, mother maybe, maybe not,
an Asian woman some thirty yards behind
who has reached the age of not hurrying
but for whom reading signs is a snap
Calls out to them, as the boy seeks her permission
saying words we cannot understand,
but one sound very much like 'go'
'Go?' he shouts
'Go!'
The girl, younger than the boy,
seizes in the frightened glee of anticipation,
her features quivering
the wonderful horror of racing across a sea of giant
hurtling machines, though of course now they are paused
waiting for the 'walk' to disappear,
like a moon behind a cloud
'Go?' she echoes, the interrogatory tone already encrypted
in her immature speech, astonished at the unsuspected gift
of so much dangerous freedom
The boy has shot in front of her, already crossed his Rubicon
The woman, still too far away, repeats her advisory, 'Go! Go!'
only now she must be hesitant lest the girl
wait too long and launch her pink wheel into danger
But she throws herself with a song, more than a squeal,
an ecstasy of embrace, of doing what her leader has done,
He is older, so that is enough
shoots across the rapid snare of danger, a blur of realized potential
triumphant for that entire instant, until the next one intervenes

Part II: Places and People

And the woman waits at the crosswalk,
no longer 'walk' but 'wait'
as the children disappear//
into//
the future

None of these three notices us
Nor, later, when couples saunter
in that imitation of oblivion
that comes because a new world shimmers beside you
and some idiot teens abandon the
girls who hang in waiting on the wall, groping
for some future knowing not yet intelligible to any of them
a language they cannot yet read,
in order (they announce, guilelessly, stupidly) to look at 'a picture of that girl'
But they are not going anywhere, that is to say
Well, not tonight

Tiny bikes, things that roll,
the parade of ceaseless machines we cannot// completely// ignore
the sidewalk is ours, and everyone's
the small yippy dogs, slower folk lounging
over bags of fried seafood-smell acquired after the epic wait
at Tony's Seafood
Small groups of women
gathering, waiting on, groups of children
of many ranged and ill-sorted ages
in bathing suits, towels, shorts and tees
the boy who throws gray sand at the back
of a brother old enough to ignore him
Until we get to the space/time
where the sun has disappeared
The darkness rising from the place where
it sleeps all day, but slowly
you can miss it, dazed by the staring at lights
that must be airplanes or tease us

Part II: Places and People

out of probability, space ships, hallucinations
Until the moon
which has been there all along
darkens to a sphinx-like smile
'who am I? where have I been?'
Knowing those below have been turning to meet him, turning
to arrive where he has always been
Infinitely// now

Part II: Places and People

Sidewalk Madonnas

("Syrian refugees registered in Lebanon make up 27 percent of the country's population." —Lebanese Interior Minister Nouhad Machnouk)

Sidewalk Madonnas
Figures of endurance
Black-robed, mourning their murdered country
Childed, uprooted, dependent on the unreliable love of strangers,
charity: rain in a dry country

They appear, a flash of darkness on a street in Hamra, back to the wall in the busy light of the Lebanese day,
The mourner at the feast,
Face hidden, grief exposed
Speaking words of the world's betrayal
distilled to an appeal we cannot hope to understand
The child you hold or sits helplessly hopeful by your side, or roams the unwelcome pavement hand outstretched,
irrefutable proof of your claim to our attention, our humanity

Our humanity is scattered, mere happenstance, thin as April sun in New England,
far from the Mediterranean blue of sky and sea
a mere trickle when a flood is needed
Where is your river, pilgrim of desperation,
your music, your song of the generations?
What rivers, borders, highways of death, bomb-shredded cities
did you leave behind with losses we cannot imagine?
Whose face will you never see again?

Women of endurance, caregivers, lifegivers from whom the future is born,
oracles of devastation ripped from your country's womb,
Tell us of the future in exchange for the slender paper note we hand you
What hope do the children of earth have
When we turn our eyes from the republic of your grief
And our backs to your violent destitution?

Part II: Places and People

My 'Little Girl Dreams'

My little girl is far away
Her milestone date, or millstone-around-the-neck date, pushed back into
that Narnian cupboard of inner space
From which, emerging like all forgotten things,
Pencil-faint scorecards from Fenway Park, tiny pink combs for dressing the
tresses of My Pretty Pony,
Lots of garlands, and sparkle, and elfy strings,
Come dreams

In my dreams I discover the little girl,
Not mine, anyone's, it's a dream so I can't remember whose I think she is,
Has been pushed aside by events
Or misunderheard so the game she had in mind
has not yet been played, though the readiness is all
I will play it
I make myself small, and listen
Now there are two of us
I will do what you want to do
If this is your dream, not mine
And even if it is mine, the same thing goes
We will go to the sandbox, or the swimming beach, or the flower garden
where you climb inside the tree circle surrounded by stella d'oro and
speedwell and coral bells and Echinacea and Pink Chablis Sedum
And plant Impatiens
I am not certain, really, whether there are flowers in my dreams
But there are surely little girls

(Will no one bring Pink Chablis to her party?)

Meanwhile, back in Beirut,
she transforms her kitchen into a fragrant, splatter-prone workshop for
making black bean burritos for her party,
rolling the tortillas in tomato sauce (is that possible?).
They hold together in the baking pan
like the world's first creatures, in love with themselves

Part II: Places and People

She makes guacamole and salsa
People come
They bring beer

They bring a huge exotic flowering plant
She answers the ring of the bell to find a giant lemon tree filling the doorway,
the secret givers like Adam and Eve lingering behind a fruit tree,
swinging like mythical forebears from the branches
The guests make a salad
They bring seven bottles of still unopened white wine

In my dream I am there
Drinking the wine (or the wind) and telling outrageous stories,
Lies mostly,
Something like this:
In my dream I dance barefoot on your table, stepping gracefully around the laptop
To prove to you that it doesn't matter, really,
Nothing does,
Except swimming lessons, bike rides, jumping the ocean waves,
Sucked out of our depth by the riptide and emerging.
Wiser but still game,
Oh, two or three decades later

And in yours the Australian woman,
Eyes blazing with antipodal effrontery,
Forces her way into your world's dirtiest kitchen,
Still gory from the black bean burrito wars,
To bake a cake from eggs and flowers and milestone ambience

And when the cake is ready your friends sing "Happy Birthday!"
Just like all the ordinary birthdays

Ah, you say, *but that really happened*
So did my dreams

Part II: Places and People

The Sacred Way

The olive trees hug the hillsides,
thick as dandelions,
while at the Monastery of Hosios Loukas
birds nest in holes left between bricks
for what conceivable purpose
but to challenge the prayers
with their ceaseless worldly note?

Frisking black goats,
their horns the shape of seashells.
their bells the sound
of centuries,
side-kick at the road side.
Who will wake Pan at his hour?

Walking with Alexander
on the sandal-smoothed steps
of The Sacred Way,
be careful not to stumble.

Part II: Places and People

Boat Ride for Mom

We should have taken this trip for you, Mom
Water so blue it pours from a paint set
You always liked the idea of a boat trip

Two hours to the first island, not Bermuda,
where white people of your generation always went
because conditions were spotlessly neat and perfect,
giving proof to that idea of perfect order you scrubbed away at
while the kids were at school

But Hydra, the motor-free pearl of the Saronic isles,
so wholly silent the shadow of a cat begging for food beneath your table
is reality's hardest knock
beyond the occasional odor of corruption from the casual enslavement of donkeys,
those ancient uncomplaining beasts of burden,
unlike you, Mother,
(or me; or anyone else I've ever known)
achieves the mark

The white of the houses, perhaps,
so glistening unworldly pure, yet the order of angels who
live there grows almonds, corruptible fruit
rising from walled gardens
and visitors dip their toes in green translucent water
reflecting the color of happiness
bathed in the light of lifted burdens,
the color of well-schooled fish feeding on chlorophyll
beneath the wands of bougainvillea
at six separate and numbered beaches
while their burdens are magically transported skyward
by those stolidly uncomplaining donkeys, uphill
on the invisible wings of mammalian patience
Like you, Mom, tackling the laundry?
...well, not really.

Part II: Places and People

How about a boat ride?
(your voice, or mine)
Wouldn't that be fun?
On board, the heartless grief-free engine submerges
the mutter of fast-moving water, molecular in its
escape from use, its eternal freedom,
and the green-capped island hills roll by
like play-things of the gods, matter left out in the rain,
or substance cooled then baked beneath the steady sun,
to the humped and mottled toes of giants

Later, after the second island,
when the sky fuzzed with haze,
like a glaze of sorrow, or regret,
reading, 'This is not the life I meant to live,'

when a mysterious mist
arises from the water,
turning the mingled shoreline of man-land and eye-land
a ghostly blue-gray,
a single pinky of white triangle in the distance
reminds me of why we have come
and why you could never come
and why the boat ride of thwarted expectations
has only a single, shadowy destination,
the unheard *aubade* to re-awakened pleasure,
and the solitary descent beneath the waves

Part II: Places and People

Old Wooden Doors
    (after a photo taken on a side street in Beirut)

What faces do we see
in the bone mirrors of long-ago trees?
A long-closed portal
to an unknowable life,
lost decades before like the city that was,
hidden beneath the mask
of an ancient plague called simply "the war."
No war now.
Merely the routine clamor
of the mind-fogging traffic.

This wall of doors has taken the veil
Patient as the ages, it watched a city crumble,
reclaim its pieces
burred with time like furred candy,
make up its face again
smile and grimace in the lightweight days of not yet summer,
a day that lets the caged bird sing
from the balcony.

No one sees you,
face of ages.
Overlooked by the steel-and-glass surgeons
who humble generations of beauty plain as day
to build walls of a different, breathless skin
that will never look
and wear a smile, Olympian,
like yours.

Part II: Places and People

Winter Comes to Quincy

Anybody know where this world is going?
On a chilly, brilliant winter night,
Chinese spices smarten up the air
The city bus hums into my sight
Ten, twelve faces frozen in the light,
The very same ones every night
A rumble from behind—the astronomical two-bus transit
Passing like ships in the night

A calligraphed tree imprints its pure shadow
On the speechless pavement, while from on high
Jupiter's gassy eye casts an unwavering gaze
On the first night of the first month of winter
Only eighty-nine such more to follow
Everything changes the same

Part II: Places and People

Waiting for the Perseids

No stars, but fire
And a guitar,
knock-knock-knocking on the soft diplomacy of clouds, visibility poor

A surge of smoke lunges like a ghost,
then twists back to the lake's black mirror
The weather worker builds a tapered temple of wood,
an offering,
draws flame from his hand

An instrument is procured for the master
The strings wind upward, songs
A few syllables hummed, rise to the diminished sky
From the dark below to the mottled cushion of the stars

The loon calls to the morning light

Part II: Places and People

My Dad's Ship But One of Three

Three ships left English port that evening
Out of sight is out of mind
Who would spy them cruising, steaming, transporting precious cargos warm
across the dark cold waters, killing North Atlantic waters
Who could see through deepest night
bodies of a breathing cargo, men and mostly young ones likewise
bound for the shore of wartime heroes, horrors, lost hurrahs
bound for the continent, La Belle France, country of culture wine,
fashionable women, les belles dames
some reduced to eating garbage left behind
by lords and masters, four long years in darkness bowed them,
liberation on its watery way

Who could see the single foe that spied them
the sea wolf banished from these waters, shark of steel,
the last survivor of the killing school that once preyed upon
both the merchant and the man-of-war,
threshed the ocean floor with seamen's bodies
till finally self on gutted self, wrapped around a deadly fish
that tumbled from the crowded lanes, a bullet in the belly from the Allied fleet,
la belle dame sans merci // offered none
All, they told us, all were gone,
Yet one shadow, evil shadow,
somehow hid its deadly eye
still patrolled the wintry waters, darkness, caverns of the sea
struck them like a water snake, poison biting through the steel
sucking down the black Atlantic into the souls of sleeping men,
infantry if not still infants, youngsters merely starting out, capped and
gowned a year, or precious merely months before,
unable still to place a vote, or have a drink in a dry home state, yet to know a woman maybe,
hoping in European harbor to find a sweet release, not a cold bed on the bottom of the sea,
Neptune's flop house, the octopus's garden, the kelp bed cafe,

Part II: Places and People

nine fathoms deep in coral bed, food for bottom feeders,
flesh for the flash of sharkish teeth, starkly laid on sea-maid's wreaths
stilled to bottom, chilled to broken, sleep no more on solid ground,
vetted in the scales of Pisces, never more sea-worthy found

One ship lost, and two survive
We are happy, we who thrive
There but for fortune, sleep you
and I

Part II: Places and People

Family Secrets

The street of the bars with private rooms
Speakeasy joints in Prohibition
Crime connections, shady roles in snap-brim hats and shady ties
My straight-shooter uncle ran a numbers game
A big shot's courier on his ice-truck route
My grandmother's resume: bar and grilles, bars with upstairs room, bars with girls.
My cousin's grandma dies upstairs
while no one calls a doctor.

All this from a friendly, family get-together
To plan the summer reunion

A lot went on, it seems, "upstairs"
While my ignorant childhood idled below
I was always happier in basements

Part II: Places and People

The Slow Tritina We Will Dance

This night we dance the harvest moon
The moon will show his private face
Deep hunger charts the busy sea

The captain marches to the sea
Its ripples silver with the glow of moon
I could not wipe from a timeless face

Remove night's glamour from your face
And wash your heart in all the sea
And still I'll see you in the moon

Your face, the moon, and the busy sea

www.ingramcontent.com/pod-product-compliance
Lightning Source LLC
LaVergne TN
LVHW041554070426
835507LV00011B/1084